THE SUN

THE SUN

SEYMOUR SIMON

MORROW JUNIOR BOOKS
New York

PHOTO CREDITS

All photographs courtesy of NASA, except pages 7 and 32,
courtesy of Kyle Cudworth, The Yerkes Observatory,
and pages 24 and 30, courtesy National Optical Astronomy Observatories.
Artwork on pages 8-9, 15, and 16 by Frank Schwartz.

Printed in Singapore by Tien Wah Press. For information address
HarperCollins Children's Books, a division of HarperCollins Publishers,
1350 Avenue of the Americas, New York, NY 10019.
www.harperchildrens.com
10   11   12   13   14   15
Library of Congress Cataloging-in-Publication Data
Simon, Seymour.
The Sun.
Summary: Describes the nature of the sun, its
origin, source of energy, layers, atmosphere, sun-
spots, and activity.
1. Sun—Juvenile literature.   [1. Sun]   I. Title.
QB521.5.S49   1986   532.7   85-32018
ISBN 0-688-05857-4 — ISBN 0-688-05858-2 (lib. bdg.)
ISBN 0-688-09236-5 (pbk.)

This book—my hundredth—is dedicated to the editors, artists, designers, production and promotion people, and all the others who have helped me beyond measure with their knowledge of the art and craft of children's books.

The sun is a star. It is a medium-sized star, but the sun appears bigger and brighter than other stars because it is so much closer to us. The sun is about 93 million miles away from Earth. The next closest star is about 25 *million million* miles away.

Although scientists can see countless stars through telescopes, the sun is the only star that they can study closely.

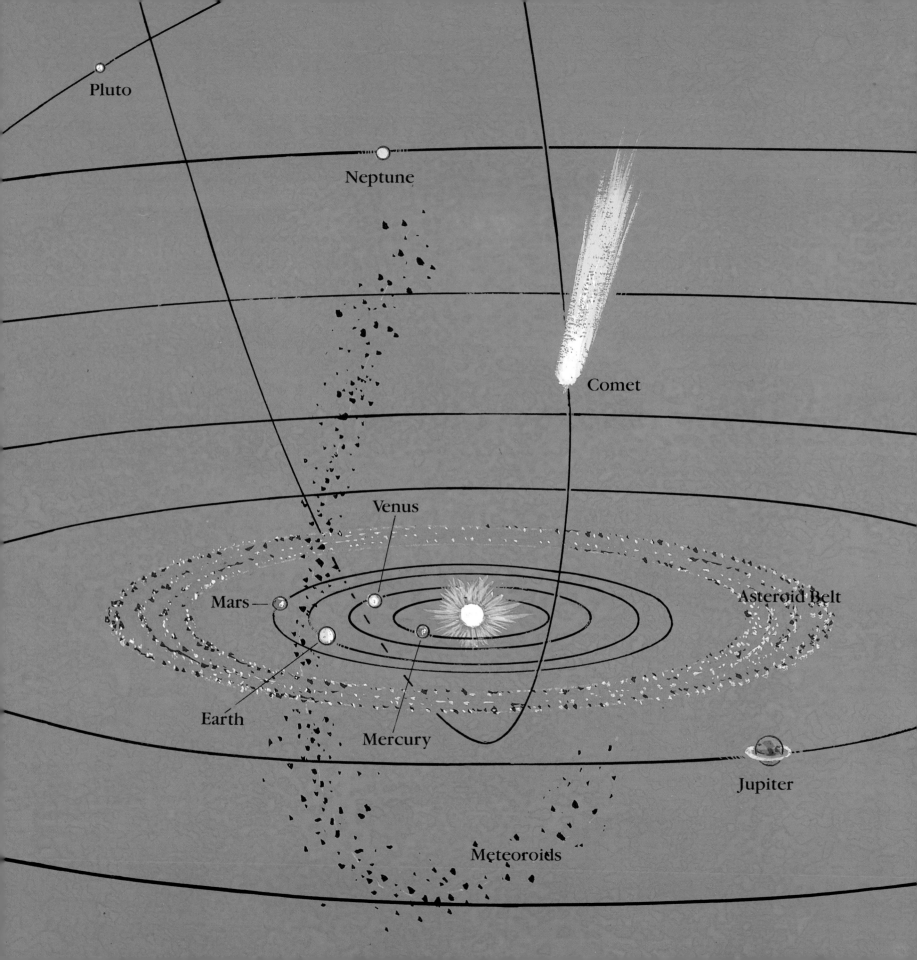

Pluto

Neptune

Comet

Venus

Mars

Asteroid Belt

Earth

Mercury

Jupiter

Meteoroids

The sun is the center of the Solar System. There are nine planets in the Solar System that travel around the sun in paths called orbits. Many of the planets have moons revolving around them. Earth is the third closest planet to the sun. Pluto is the most distant planet, almost four billion miles from the sun. From faraway Pluto, the sun looks only like a bright star in a dark sky.

There are thousands of minor planets, called asteroids, that orbit the sun. These lumps of rock, which range in size from pebbles to nearly five hundred miles across, circle the sun in a broad "asteroid belt" between the orbits of the planets Mars and Jupiter. Many smaller rocks called meteoroids also travel around the sun. Finally, there are many comets orbiting the sun. Comets are clumps of ice and dust that begin to glow and produce shining tails when they come near the sun.

Saturn

Uranus

The sun is huge compared to Earth. If the sun were hollow it could hold 1.3 *million* Earths. Think of this: If Earth were the size of a golf ball, then the sun would be a globe about fifteen feet across. In fact, the sun is nearly 600 times bigger than all the planets in the Solar System put together.

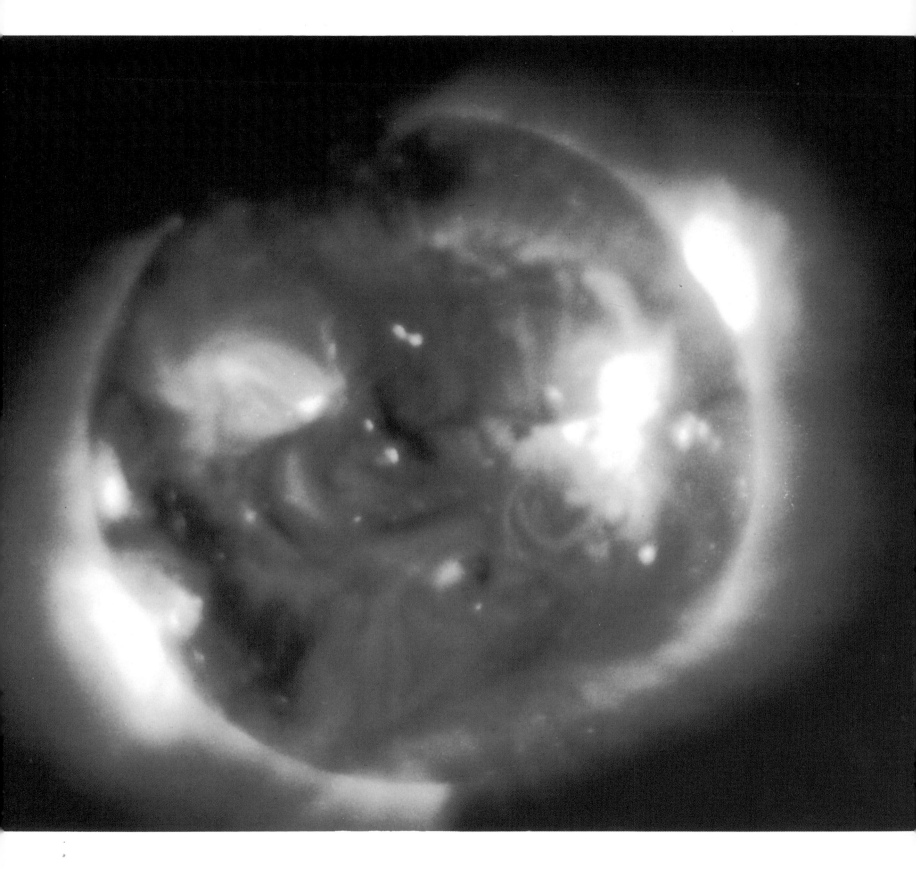

The sun's light and heat come from fires deep within it. But the sun doesn't burn in the same way as a fire does on Earth. If the sun were just a huge bonfire it would have burned out long ago. Instead the sun is more like an endless hydrogen bomb.

About five billion years ago, a huge cloud of dust and hydrogen gas began to pull together forming a globe. As the gas and dust packed together more and more tightly, the globe became hotter and hotter. Finally, the globe became hot enough to set off a chain of nuclear explosions and the sun began to shine. These explosions are still going on.

Hydrogen is the sun's "fuel." The sun uses about four million tons of hydrogen every second. Still, the sun has enough hydrogen to continue shining for another five billion years.

What is it like inside the sun? Of course, no spaceship could travel there. Every material we know would be instantly destroyed by the intense heat. But let's use the spaceship of our mind to explore the sun.

At the very center of the sun is its core. The sun's core is about as big as the planet Jupiter, about one hundred thousand miles across. Here, constant nuclear explosions turn hydrogen gas into invisible X-ray energy. Temperatures in the core may reach as high as 27 million degrees (F).

Around the core are two layers, the radiative zone and the convective zone, which make up most of the sun's interior. Here X rays from the core move outward toward the surface. Normally, these rays move at the speed of light — 186,000 miles per second. But inside the sun, X rays are greatly slowed down by the tightly packed gases. It takes an X ray millions of years to reach the sun's surface.

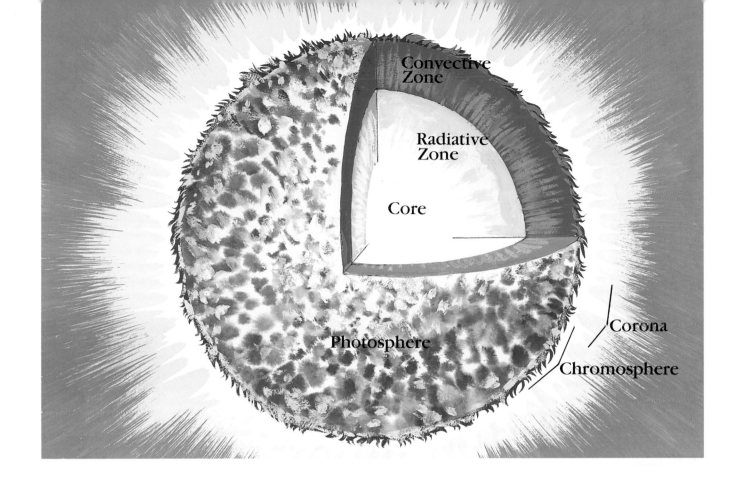

The photosphere is a sea of boiling gases that makes up the sun's surface. The photosphere (*photo* means "light") is what we see when we look at the sun in the sky. (WARNING: Never look directly at the sun. The direct rays of the sun can injure your eyes.) The temperature of the photosphere is about 10 thousand degrees (F). But there are some hotter areas that form on the surface, just like bubbles in boiling water.

Like Earth, the sun has an atmosphere, a cloud of gases, surrounding it. The sun's inner atmosphere is called the chromosphere (*chromo* means "color"). We usually can't see the chromosphere because it is hidden in the bright glare of the sun's surface. However, the chromosphere does become visible during a total eclipse of the sun. A solar eclipse takes place when the moon comes between Earth and the sun, blocking out light from the sun. For a few minutes, only the sun's atmosphere is visible.

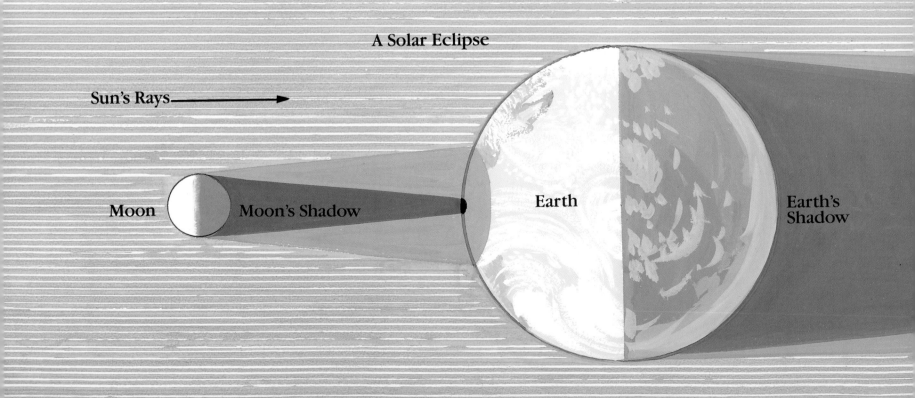

A Solar Eclipse

Sun's Rays

Moon

Moon's Shadow

Earth

Earth's Shadow

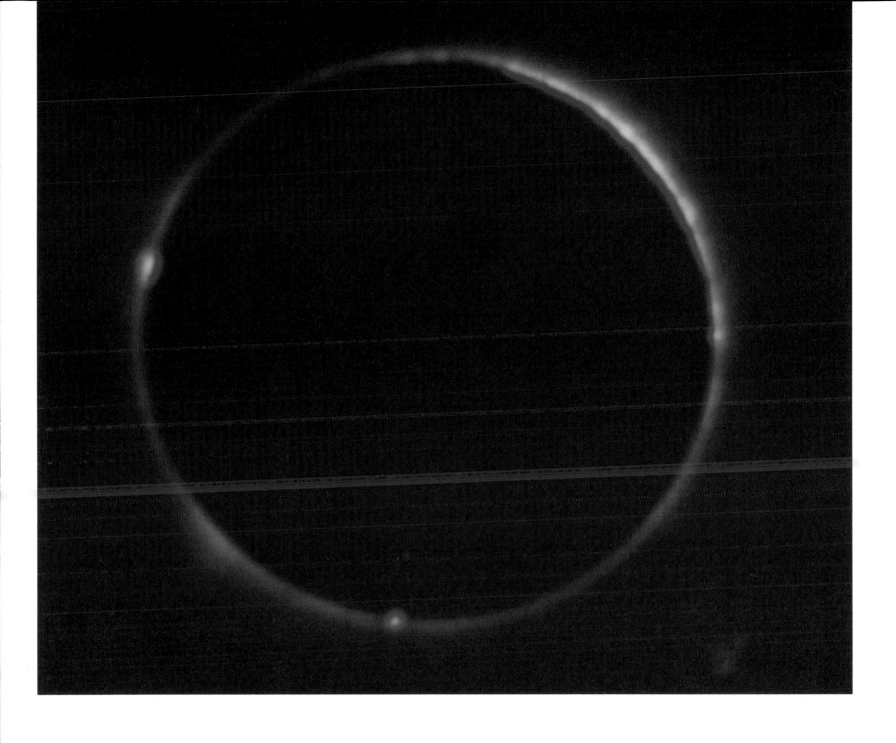

This photo of a solar eclipse shows the pink layer of the chromosphere shining around the moon's dark disc.

Surrounding the chromosphere is the sun's outer atmosphere, the corona. The sun's corona is made up of thin gases that are very, very hot, almost 3 million degrees (F).

The corona stretches outward for millions of miles into space. During a total solar eclipse, the corona is visible as a halo or crown of light around the sun (*corona* means "crown").

Scientists have discovered another way to study the sun's corona. They use a *corona-graph*, an instrument that blocks out the sun's surface. This allows them to photo-graph and study the corona over a long period of time, not just for the few minutes of a solar eclipse.

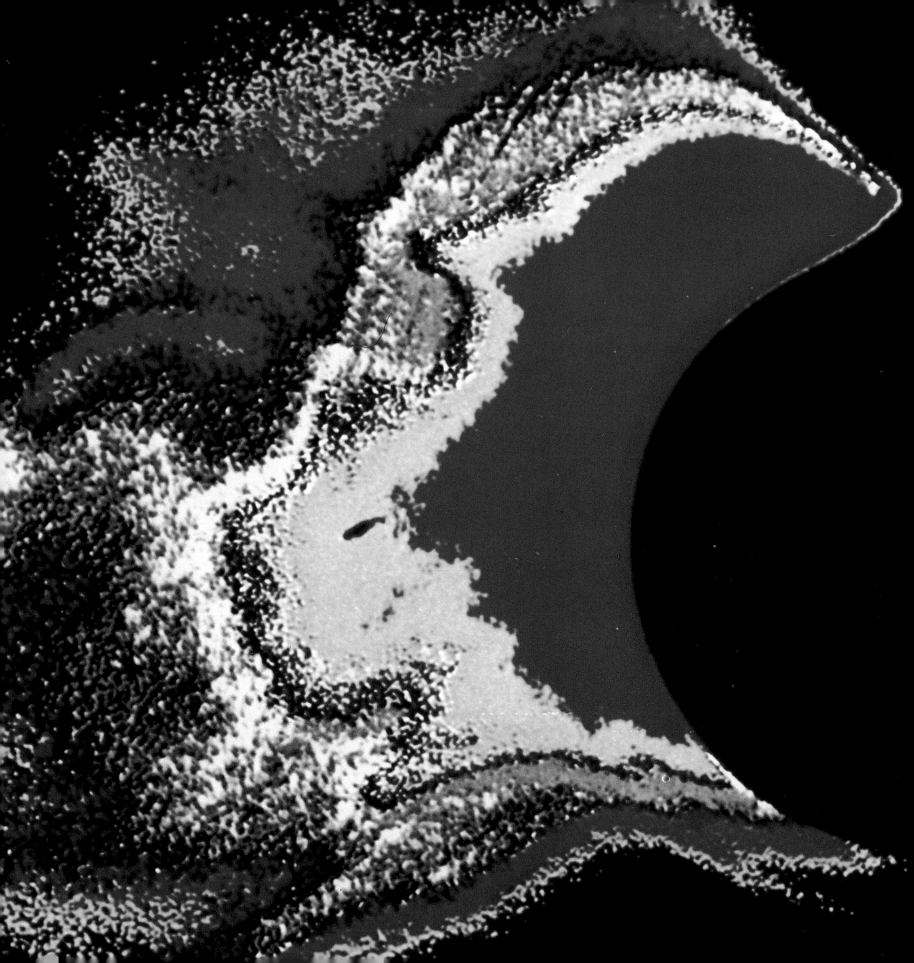

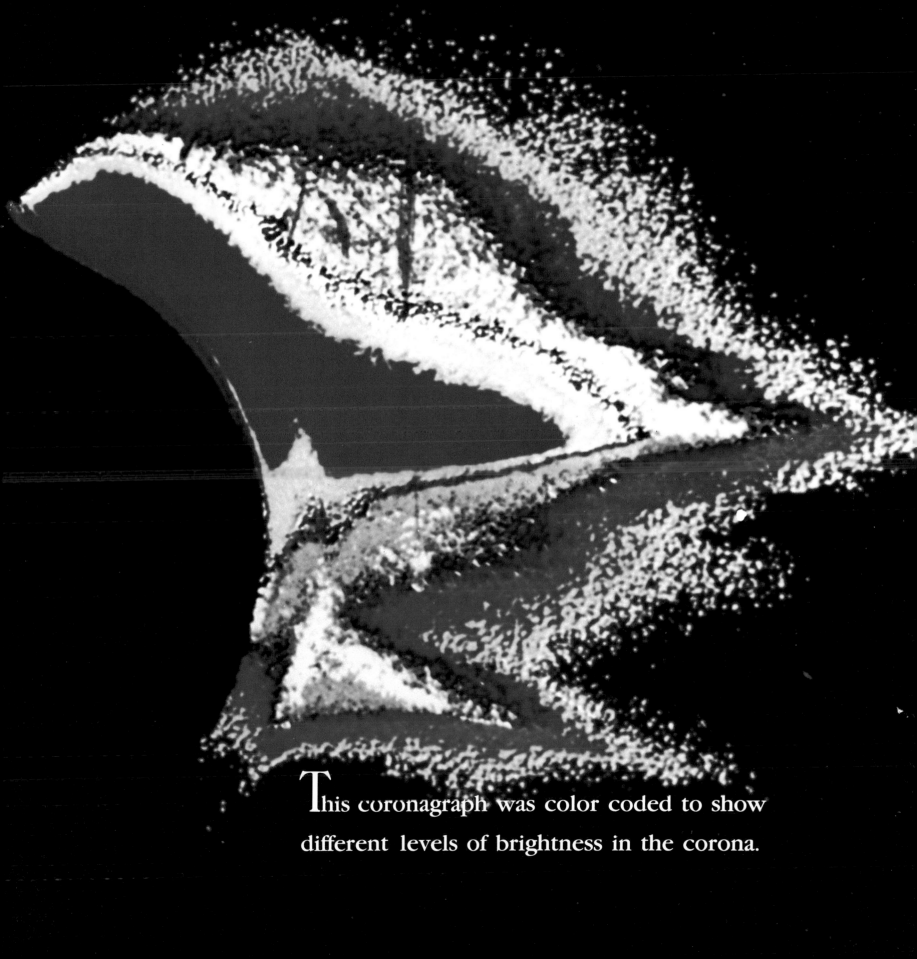

This coronagraph was color coded to show different levels of brightness in the corona.

The sun is never at rest. Sometimes giant storms called sunspots erupt on the surface. These storms look like dark spots or blotches. The line of sunspots in the lower part of this photograph is a storm one hundred thousand miles across, twelve times wider than Earth.

Sunspots send powerful streams of electrical energy into space. The energy released in one hour by this one storm is equal to all of the electrical power that probably will be used in the United States over the next million years!

The numbers of sunspots change over an eleven-year period called the sunspot cycle. During a year when the sun is quiet, large sunspots appear very rarely. During a year when the sun is active, as many as one hundred large sunspots appear. The next peak in the sunspot cycle should occur about 1991.

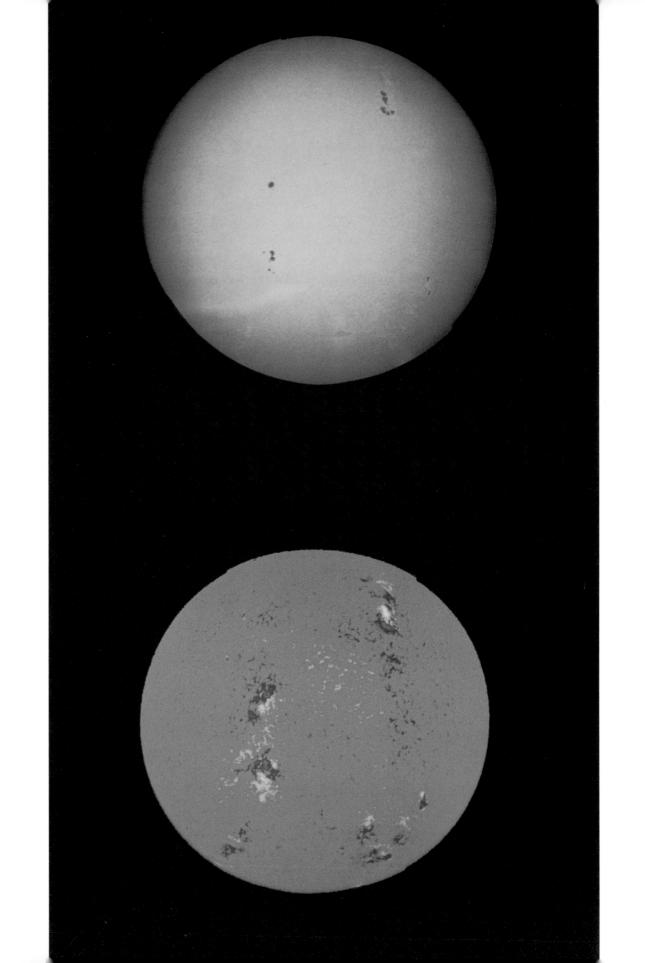

What causes sunspots? Scientists are not exactly sure. They do know that the sun is like a giant magnet with north and south magnetic poles. Scientists think that sunspots occur when powerful magnetic storms break out on the sun's surface and prevent some heat and light from escaping. That's why the spots are darker than their surroundings.

This photo shows two views of the same sunspot activity. The picture on the bottom is called a magnetogram. It shows that each pair of sunspots has both a north and south pole. A magnetic force over one thousand times stronger than normal runs between them and stretches in a loop up into the sun's atmosphere.

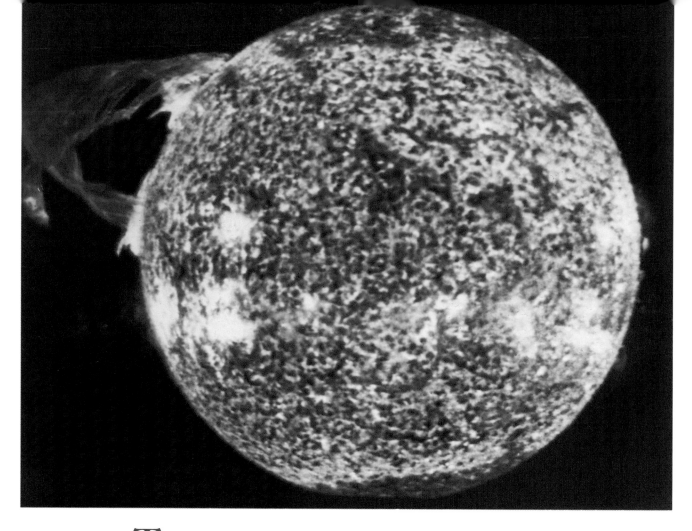

The magnetic forces erupting out of sun-spots sometimes carry hot gases with them. These flaming streams of gas are called prominences. Traveling at speeds up to 200 miles per second, prominences arch up through the sun's atmosphere.

Some prominences fly off into space, but

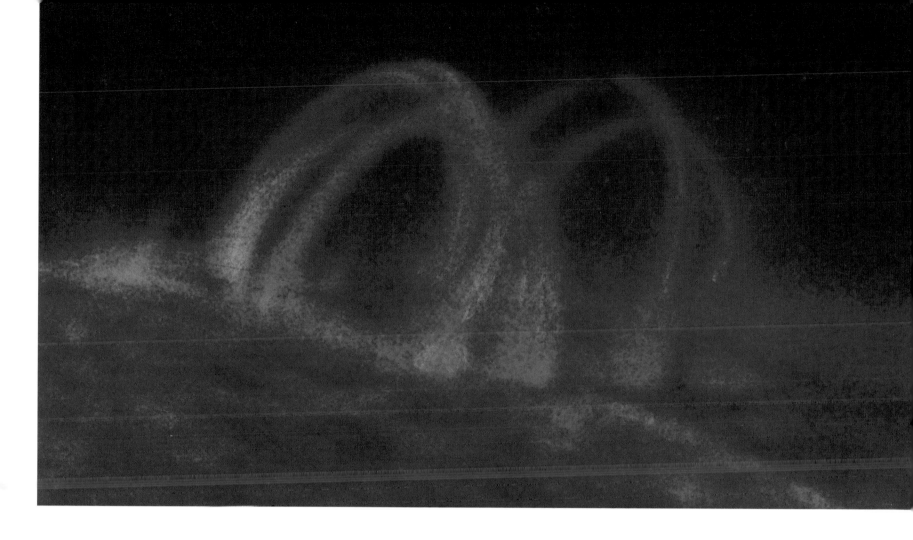

most loop back to the sun. Many prominences are over 100 thousand miles long and 3,000 miles thick, yet they can rise and fall in just a few hours. Other prominences last for days or even weeks. This photograph shows the magnetic loops that carry the hot gases of prominences.

Sometimes the magnetic forces in a large sunspot are released in fiery explosions called flares. Flares last for only a few minutes, yet can have the power of ten million hydrogen bombs. These violent explosions send out waves of intense heat, light, and radiation. When this radiation hits Earth a few hours later, it can black out communications and cause the magnetic compasses on airplanes and ships to spin wildly for a short time.

Flares also send out great numbers of tiny particles out into space. Some of these particles reach Earth and become trapped in Earth's magnetic field near the North and South Poles. As these particles come down through our atmosphere they make the air glow in shimmering multi-colored curtains of light called auroras. In the north this is called the aurora borealis or northern lights. In the south it is called the aurora australis or southern lights.

The sun is all important to life on Earth. Our weather and climate depend upon the sun. Green plants need sunlight to grow. Animals eat plants for food, and we need plants and animals to live. Even the fuels we use such as coal, oil, and gas are the remains of once-living things. Without the sun there would be no heat, no light, no clouds, no rain — no living thing on Earth.